The Three Little Pigs

retold by Mark Lewis
illustrated by Nancy Speir

Harcourt
SCHOOL PUBLISHERS

Printed in China

ISBN 10: 0-15-350017-4
ISBN 13: 978-0-15-350017-6

Ordering Options
ISBN 10: 0-15-349938-9 (Grade 3 ELL Collection)
ISBN 13: 978-0-15-349938-8 (Grade 3 ELL Collection)
ISBN 10: 0-15-357256-6 (package of 5)
ISBN 13: 978-0-15-357256-2 (package of 5)

3 4 5 6 7 8 9 10 985 12 11 10 09 08

Once upon a time, there were three little pigs. They played together all summer, but then the days started to get cool. The three pigs knew it was time to build a house for winter. They couldn't agree on how to build the house, so each pig built his own house.

One pig was lazy, so he decided to build a straw house. "My house will only take a day to build," he said.

"Your house definitely will not be strong enough," stated his brothers.

"I will build it my way," replied the first pig. In one day he had made his house, and he went outside to play.

The second pig planned to build a wooden house. "My house will only take three days to build," he said.

"Your house definitely will not be strong enough," stated the wise pig.

"I will build it my way," replied the second pig. In three days he had made his house, and he went outside to play.

The third little pig was extremely wise. "A good house must be strong," he said. "It must protect me from the wolf! That's why I will build a brick house."

"You are just wasting your time," said his brothers, who then went to play.

"I will build it my way," replied the wise pig. He worked hard for many days, and he built a strong house.

One day, the pigs noticed wolf tracks. Each pig rushed to his own house.

The hungry wolf arrived at the straw house. "Come out, little pig! I want to speak with you!" howled the wolf.

"Go away," shouted the lazy pig.

"I will make you come out!" growled
the wolf. The wolf took a deep breath
and blew as hard as he could.

The straw house fell down. The
lazy pig ran as fast as he could to his
brother's house that was made of wood.

The wolf ran after the lazy pig, but
he was already inside his brother's
wooden house.

The wolf was growing hungrier.
"Open up! I want to talk!" howled
the wolf.

"Go away!" the brothers called.

"I will make you come out!" roared the wolf. He took a deep breath, and he blew as hard as he could.

The wooden house fell down. The two little pigs ran as fast as they could to their brother's brick house. The wise little pig let his brothers in, and he quickly shut the door.

The wolf came to the wise pig's house. The wolf blew and blew as hard as he could, but the brick house did not fall. Then the wolf climbed up to the roof and began to lower himself down the chimney.

"We'll build a nice fire," said the wise pig. When the wolf felt the heat of the fire, he knew he could not go down the chimney. The wolf ran away into the forest.

The three little pigs were very happy. They danced and sang in the yard.

The two lazy pigs started working that same day. They each built a strong new brick house.

One day, the wolf came back to the pigs' neighborhood. When he saw the three brick houses, the wolf ran away. He never bothered the pigs again!